THE ULTIMATE
MANCHESTER CITY FC
TRIVIA BOOK

A Collection of Amazing Trivia Quizzes
and Fun Facts for Die-Hard City Fans!

Ray Walker

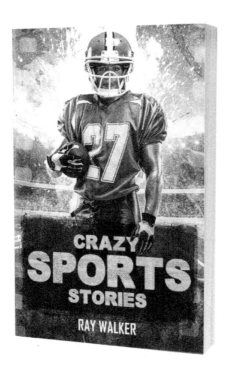

CONTENTS

INTRODUCTION

The Manchester City soccer club was originally formed just over 140 years ago as St. Mark's, and then evolved into Ardwick AFC, before finally settling on Manchester City FC. The side has survived two World Wars and several lean years and relegations to become one of the strongest and richest clubs in the world.

Known by several nicknames, the team has one of the most passionate fan bases in the world of sports. Supporters stuck with the club when silverware was hard to come by and their loyalty is paying off handsomely now, as City has become a powerhouse in the UK, and Europe, over the past couple of decades.

There's still more to shoot for, though, because the elusive European Cup Champions League title has yet to be won. City owns several league and British records, but nobody is prepared to rest on their laurels. Fans can still remember the team being forced to play in England's third tier of football and they realize what it takes to prevent it from happening again.

There's no denying that City has been on the ropes several times during its history, but the club has always battled back.

City supporters have had the pleasure of witnessing some of the world's greatest players suit up for their side over the years, as well as enjoying the tactics of some of the most successful managers. Who could forget the likes of Sergio Agüero, Colin Bell, Eric Brook Mike Summerbee, Shaun Wright-Phillips, Kolo, and Yaya Touré, Joe Hart, Kevin De Bruyne, Vincent Kompany, Billy Meredith, Richard Dunne, David Silva, Stuart Pearce, Kevin Keegan, Joe Mercer, or Pep Guardiola?

This lighthearted trivia and fact book has recently been put together to celebrate the club's remarkable persistence and history over almost a century and a half.

You'll be able to relive the dramatic and disappointing moments from day one until 2021. You'll be reminded of the squad's most beloved characters and how each of them influenced the club in their own way.

Man City's intriguing history is presented here in quiz form with 12 different unique chapters. Each chapter contains 20 challenging quiz questions along with 10 educational "Did You Know" facts. The questions are presented in 15 multiple-choice and 5 true-or-false options with the answers available on a separate page.

We feel this is the ideal tool to challenge yourself on the club's history and to prepare yourself for all Man City quiz and trivia challenges that come your way.

CHAPTER 1:

ORIGINS & HISTORY

QUIZ TIME!

1. In what year was the club founded?

   a. 1901

   b. 1889

   c. 1880

   d. 1876

2. Man City was founded as St. Mark's (West Gorton).

   a. True

   b. False

3. Who did the club play its first-ever friendly match against?

   a. Macclesfield

   b. Burton Swifts FC

   c. St. Andrews Athletics

   d. Lincoln City

4. Which of the following men was not one of the key founders of the club?

   a. Arthur Connell

   b. Scottie McDowell

   c. William Beastow

   d. Thomas Goodbehere

5. What was the first league the team joined?

   a. Manchester League

   b. The Combination

   c. The Football League

   d. Football Alliance

6. What was the club's name before officially changing it to Manchester City in 1894?

   a. Manchester AFC

   b. Bradford FC

   c. West Gorton Footballers

   d. Ardwick AFC

7. Man City has worn a sky-blue jersey since 1894.

   a. True

   b. False

8. What was the original crest design of the club?

   a. The Manchester coat of arms

   b. A white cross

   c. A shield in a circle

   d. Three roses and a sword

9. What was the final score of the team's first friendly match?

    a. 1-0 win
    b. 2-2 draw
    c. 2-1 loss
    d. 3-0 win

10. How many times has Man City been relegated as of 2020?

    a. 5
    b. 8
    c. 11
    d. 14

11. Man City played its first official league match against which club?

    a. Bootle FC
    b. Newton Heath
    c. Grimsby Town
    d. Crewe Alexandra

12. Man City did not play in the inaugural season of the Premier League.

    a. True
    b. False

13. What was the squad's original shirt color?

    a. Black
    b. Red
    c. Royal Blue
    d. White with a red pin stripe

14. In which year was Man City first relegated?

    a. 1949-50
    b. 1937-38
    c. 1925-26
    d. 1901-02

15. Who scored Man City's first goal in the Premier League?

    a. Niall Quinn
    b. Stephen McMahon
    c. David White
    d. Fitzroy Simpson

16. Man City was promoted to the First Division in 1902-03.

    a. True
    b. False

17. Man City's first Premier League match was a 1-1 draw against which club?

    a. Middlesbrough FC
    b. Queens Park Rangers
    c. Oldham Athletic
    d. Chelsea FC

18. Where did the club play its home matches beginning in 1887?

    a. Hyde Road
    b. Ardwick Stadium
    c. Maine Road
    d. City of Manchester Stadium

19. What was the first club Man City defeated in the Premier League?

    a. Sheffield Wednesday

    b. Arsenal FC

    c. Crystal Palace

    d. Norwich City FC

20. Man City won its first major trophy in 1904.

    a. True

    b. False

QUIZ ANSWERS

1. C – 1880

2. A – True

3. A – Macclesfield

4. B – Scottie McDowell

5. D – Football Alliance

6. D – Ardwick AFC

7. A – True

8. B – White Cross

9. C – 2-1 loss

10. C – 11

11. A – Bootle FC

12. B – False

13. A – Black

14. D – 1901-02

15. C – David White

16. B – False

17. B – Queens Park Rangers

18. A – Hyde Road

19. D – Norwich City FC

20. A – True

DID YOU KNOW?

1. Manchester City FC is based in Manchester, England, and currently competes in that country's top-flight division, the Premier League. The team plays its home games at the Etihad Stadium, and the club's nicknames are City, Man City, Cityzens, the Citizens, the Sky Blues, and MCFC, with some fans just calling the team the Blues. The fans' song of choice at home games is "Blue Moon."

2. The roots of Manchester City can be traced back to 1880 when the club began as a church team known as St. Mark's (West Gorton), and then became the Ardwick Association Football Club in 1887, playing its home games at Hyde Road.

3. In 1875, a church cricket club was formed but there were no activities for the winter months. Rector Arthur Connell, along with his daughter Anna and church wardens William Beastow and Thomas Goodbehere, then formed a church football team to keep people active in the winter of 1880. The team's first recorded game took place on Nov. 13, 1880, against a church side from Macclesfield, with St. Mark's losing 2-1.

4. The Second Division of the English Football League was created in 1892 and Ardwick AFC was one of the founding members. Ardwick AFC was then officially renamed the Manchester City Football Club in April 1894.

Man City won the Division Two championship in 1898-99, becoming the first team to earn automatic promotion to the First Division.

5. The first known team shirt in 1884 was black and featured a white Maltese-style cross. It's believed this may have been because of the club's strong links to Freemasonry at the time. However, others feel the cross was because of the strong links with St Mark's. The club then chose sky blue home shirts in 1894; the colors are still in use in 2021.

6. The outfit won its first major trophy in 1904 by capturing the FA Cup with a win over Bolton Wanderers and captured its first First Division title in 1936-37. The club's first major successful period came 60 years later when it won the First Division, European Cup Winners Cup, FA Cup, and League Cup, with managers Joe Mercer and Malcolm Allison at the helm.

7. Following defeat in the 1981 FA Cup final, Man City struggled for several years and was relegated to the third tier of English football in 1997-1998 for the first and only time so far. The side earned promotion back to the top flight in 2001-02 and has played in the Premier League continuously since 2002–03.

8. The team played its home matches at Maine Road stadium from 1923 to 2003 when it moved to the City of Manchester Stadium in east Manchester. However, due to naming rights, the venue is currently known as the Etihad Stadium.

9. In 2008, the Abu Dhabi United Group purchased Man City for £210 million, which included club facilities, playing staff, and the Etihad Campus in East Manchester. The club is currently owned by the City Football Group, a British-based holding company. The Abu Dhabi United Group holds 78 percent of the shares.

10. With Pep Guardiola as manager, the side won the 2017-18 Premier League and became the first team in the division to post 100 points in a season. In 2018-19, the outfit claimed four different trophies, including all domestic titles, becoming the first English men's squad to win the domestic treble of the league, League Cup, and FA Cup.

CHAPTER 2:

THE CAPTAIN CLASS

QUIZ TIME!

1. Which club did skipper Paul Power join in 1986 after leaving Man City?

    a. Norwich City FC

    b. Everton FC

    c. Fulham FC

    d. Leeds United

2. Man City has had 87 full-time captains as of 2020.

    a. True

    b. False

3. Which player won the club's Player of the Year award four times?

    a. Kolo Touré

    b. Sylvain Distin

    c. Richard Dunne

    d. Kevin De Bruyne

4. Who was named captain in September 2020?

    a. Raheem Sterling
    b. Kevin De Bruyne
    c. Sergio Agüero
    d. Fernandinho

5. How many trophies did Tony Book lead Man City to?

    a. 7
    b. 4
    c. 1
    d. 3

6. Who captained Man City to its first FA Cup win in 1903-04?

    a. Billy Meredith
    b. Joe Cassidy
    c. Billie Gillespie
    d. Di Jones

7. Max Woosnam is often referred to as the "greatest British sportsman."

    a. True
    b. False

8. Andy Morrison was acquired for £80,000 from which club?

    a. Plymouth Argyle
    b. Sheffield United
    c. Huddersfield Town AFC
    d. Blackpool FC

9. Who succeeded Carlos Tevez as captain?

   a. Owen Hargreaves
   b. Kolo Touré
   c. Nigel de Jong
   d. Vincent Kompany

10. How old was Tony Book when he joined Man City?

   a. 19
   b. 24
   c. 28
   d. 31

11. Vincent Kompany was named captain of which club after leaving Man City?

   a. Hamburger SV
   b. RSC Anderlecht
   c. Antwerp FC
   d. Standard Liège

12. Billy Meredith was one of several players suspended in 1906 after allegations about the club's handling of finances.

   a. True
   b. False

13. Which player did Fernandinho succeed as captain?

   a. David Silva
   b. Vincent Kompany
   c. İlkay Gündoğan
   d. Sergio Agüero

14. Which club did Carlos Tevez join Man City from?

    a. CA Boca Juniors
    b. West Ham United
    c. Manchester United
    d. SC Corinthians Paulista

15. Which athletic feat did Max Woosnam not perform?

    a. He won a gold medal in doubles tennis at the 1920 Olympic Games.
    b. He captained England's national soccer team.
    c. He set a record for most stolen bases in a season in the British Baseball Federation.
    d. He compiled a break of 147 in snooker.

16. Davie Weir was the club's first captain in the Football Alliance.

    a. True
    b. False

17. Who did Richard Dunne succeed as captain?

    a. Stuart Pearce
    b. Sylvain Distin
    c. Andy Morrison
    d. Darius Vassell

18. Which player captained Man City to the 1956 FA Cup final?

    a. Roy Little
    b. Jack Dyson
    c. Roy Paul
    d. Ken Barnes

19. From which team did Stuart Pearce join Man City?

    a. Nottingham Forest
    b. Coventry City FC
    c. Newcastle United
    d. West Ham United

20. Stuart Pearce captained Man City in his only season with the squad.

    a. True
    b. False

QUIZ ANSWERS

1. B – Everton FC

2. B – False

3. C – Richard Dunne

4. D – Fernandinho

5. B – 4

6. A – Billy Meredith

7. A – True

8. C – Huddersfield Town AFC

9. D – Vincent Kompany

10. D – 31

11. B – RSC Anderlecht

12. A – True

13. A – David Silva

14. C – Manchester United

15. C – He set a record for most stolen bases in a season in the British Baseball Federation.

16. B – False

17. B – Sylvain Distin

18. C – Roy Paul

19. D – West Ham United

20. A – True

DID YOU KNOW?

1. Dozens of players have worn the captain's armband for Man City since the club was formed, some as full-time appointees and others acting as part-time or temporary skippers. In recent years, the club has allowed its players and staff to vote on the captain and vice-captain positions rather than having team management simply hand the armband to a player.

2. Brazilian international defender and midfielder Fernandinho was chosen by the Man City players and staff to be the club's full-time captain for the 2020-21 season and Kevin De Bruyne was elected to act as vice-captain. Fernandinho took over the armband from Spanish international David Silva, who joined Real Sociedad after spending a decade with City. Fernandinho has played over 300 games for the club as of February 2021 and has helped to win nine major trophies.

3. Defender and midfielder Paul Power joined the club in 1975 and played over 440 games, being appointed skipper in 1979. He'll never be forgotten for his play in the team's run to the 1980-1981 FA Cup final, which City lost in a replay to Tottenham Hotspur. He also led the squad to the League Cup semifinal that campaign. Power played three cup finals at Wembley and in 1984-85 led the side to promotion from the second tier. He was named Man City

Player of the Year for 1980-81 and 1984-85. Power joined Everton in 1986 and won a league title with the club. Known for his leadership and professionalism, he later rejoined City as an academy coach.

4. Richard Dunne won Man City's Player of the Year award four times after the defender arrived from Everton in 2000 and became an instant fan favorite. Manager Kevin Keegan suspended him in 2003 for disciplinary reasons and the public humiliation worked out well for Dunne as he returned with a more professional attitude and was named captain in the summer of 2006. He played over 350 games with the team, helping it win the second-tier First Division in 2001-02, before joining Aston Villa in 2009. The Irish international played over 500 league games in his career and currently shares the Premier League record for being sent off eight times. He also owns the league's record for scoring 10 goals against his own team.

5. Andy Morrison arrived at the right time for Man City in 1998-99 because the club was desperately seeking on-pitch leadership after being relegated to the third-tier Second Division. Costing just £80,000 from Huddersfield Town, He helped the team earn promotion in his first season by leading it to a victory in the Second Division playoffs. The next season, City earned promotion to the Premier League by finishing as First Division runners-up, only to be relegated after one season. Oddly enough, although Morrison is considered to be one of City's greatest captains, injuries and being sent on loan limited him to

just under 50 appearances. He later returned to the club as a fan ambassador.

6. Welsh international defender Roy Paul played just under 300 games with Man City between 1950 and 1957 after arriving from Swansea Town and before joining Worcester City. After City was relegated, Paul was acquired for £19,500 to set a British record for a half-back. The skipper led his side to successive FA Cup finals in 1954-55 and 1955-1956, with a defeat by Newcastle United in the first match and a victory over Birmingham City in the second. Known for his physical strength and inspiring leadership tactics, Paul was a member of the Worcester team that famously knocked Liverpool out of the FA Cup in 1959.

7. Vincent Kompany was signed from Hamburger SV in 2008 by manager Mark Hughes for a reported £6 million and cemented himself as one of the team's best defenders and captains ever, winning the club's Player of the Year award in 2011. The Belgian international captained the squad to its first top-flight league title in 44 years in 2011-12. He won three more Premier League titles, as well as two FA Cups, four League Cups, and a pair of FA Community Shields. In addition, Kompany was named the club's Official Supporter's Player of the Year for 2010-11 and the Premier League Player of the Season for 2011-12. He was also named to the PFA Premier League Team of the Year three times. Kompany played over 350 times and netted 20 goals for the club before joining Anderlecht in 2019.

8. Tony Book finished his pro career with Man City from 1966 to 1974 after joining from Plymouth Argyle. He captained the team to four major trophies: a league title in 1967-68, the FA Cup in 1968-69, the European Cup Winners' Cup in 1969-1970, and the League Cup in 1969-70. He played for non-league Bath until the age of 28, then played in Canada with Toronto City before joining Plymouth and making his Football League debut as a 30-year-old. After hanging up his boots, Book managed City, was named honorary president of the club and life president of the Man City Official Supporters Club, and was inducted into the team's hall of fame.

9. After spending his youth career with Man City defender and midfielder Mike Doyle played with the first team from 1965 to 1978 before joining Stoke City. Doyle played 570 games with the club and chipped in with over 40 goals. The club's official magazine voted Doyle the team's hardest-ever player and he captained the squad in the 1975-1976 League Cup final. Doyle helped his teammates win eight trophies at City, including a First and Second Division title, two League Cups, an FA Cup, and the European Cup Winners' Cup. He was also named Man City Player of the Year for 1971 and 1974.

10. In 2009, defender Kolo Touré arrived from Arsenal and had an immediate impact, as City captured the Premier League crown in 2011-12. He's currently the second most-capped player for the Ivory Coast at 120 appearances and holds the record for an African player in the Premier

League with 353 appearances. He remained with City until leaving for Liverpool in 2013. Touré played 102 games with City and also helped the team win the 2012 FA Community Shield while contributing 3 goals. As of 2021, he was a first-team coach with Leicester City.

CHAPTER 3:

AMAZING MANAGERS

QUIZ TIME!

1. Who was the club's first known full-time manager?

    a. Frederick Hopkinson

    b. Lawrence Furniss

    c. Joshua Parlby

    d. David Ashworth

2. During the Football League era, Man City had approximately 21 full-time managers.

    a. True

    b. False

3. Pep Guardiola succeeded which of these managers?

    a. Roberto Mancini

    b. Mark Hughes

    c. Sven-Göran Eriksson

    d. Manuel Pellegrini

4. Which club did Peter Reid manage after leaving Man City?

    a. Leeds United

    b. Coventry City FC

    c. Sunderland AFC

    d. Plymouth Argyle

5. Who managed the side to its first-ever league title in the Second Division?

    a. Tom Maley

    b. Harry Newbould

    c. Sam Ormerod

    d. Peter Hodge

6. Which manager guided the club to its first top-flight title?

    a. Joe Mercer

    b. Wilf Wild

    c. Tom Maley

    d. Jock Thompson

7. Wilf Wild is currently recognized as the club's longest-serving manager by years.

    a. True

    b. False

8. Who succeeded Joe Mercer as manager?

    a. Johnny Hart

    b. Malcolm Allison

    c. Ron Saunders

    d. John Bond

9. Pep Guardiola managed which club before joining Man City?

    a. FC Barcelona

    b. AC Milan

    c. Bayern Munich

    d. FC Porto

10. Who succeeded Jimmy Frizzell as manager?

    a. Mel Machin

    b. Howard Kendall

    c. Billy McNeil

    d. Peter Reid

11. Who is the club's most successful manager as of 2020 in terms of trophies won?

    a. Joe Mercer

    b. Pep Guardiola

    c. Les McDowall

    d. Roberto Mancini

12. Sven-Göran Eriksson was the club's first manager who was born in Sweden.

    a. True

    b. False

13. How many trophies did Joe Mercer win with Man City?

    a. 3

    b. 5

    c. 8

    d. 12

14. Which club did Roberto Mancini manage before joining Man City?

    a. Borussia Dortmund
    b. S.S. Lazio
    c. Liverpool FC
    d. Inter Milan

15. How many trophies has Pep Guardiola won with the team as of 2020?

    a. 13
    b. 10
    c. 8
    d. 6

16. Tony Book became the first person to win the League Cup as a player and manager.

    a. True
    b. False

17. Who managed the side in its first Premier League campaign?

    a. Tony Book
    b. Brian Horton
    c. Peter Reid
    d. Howard Kendall

18. Who became manager after Sven-Göran Eriksson left Man City?

    a. Kevin Keegan
    b. Robert Mancini

c. Mark Hughes

d. Stuart Pearce

19. How many trophies did Wilf Wild win while managing Man City?

a. 7

b. 1

c. 5

d. 3

20. Man City has had three Canadian-born managers.

a. True

b. False

QUIZ ANSWERS

1. A – Frederick Hopkinson

2. B – False

3. D – Manuel Pellegrini

4. C – Sunderland AFC

5. C – Sam Ormerod

6. B – Wilf Wild

7. A – True

8. B – Malcolm Allison

9. C – Bayern Munich

10. A – Mel Machin

11. B – Pep Guardiola

12. A – True

13. B – 5

14. D – Inter Milan

15. C – 8

16. A – True

17. C – Peter Reid

18. C – Mark Hughes

19. D – 3

20. B – False

DID YOU KNOW?

1. Including the West Gorton (St. Mark's) and Ardwick teams before the club became Manchester City, there have been approximately 34 managers for the side during the Football League era, which began in 1888-89. When pre-league managers and temporary caretakers are taken into account, the number swells to over 40. The first known manager was Frederick Hopkinson of England between 1880 and 1882. As of February 2021, the current boss was Pep Guardiola of Spain, who was appointed on July 1, 2016.

2. The longest-serving Man City manager was Wilf Wild. However, Les McDowall was in charge of the team for the most competitive games, with Wild ranking second. That's because Wild's stint included several years during World War II when league football was put on hold in England. When it comes to winning silverware, Pep Guardiola has been the most successful boss.

3. The first manager of the Football League era was Lawrence Furniss, who reportedly held the position from August 1889 to May 1893. He was a key member of the St. Mark's congregation and played for its soccer team. After hanging up his boots, he took on an administrative role and helped in the development of the Hyde Road and Maine Road stadiums. He became secretary-manager of

Ardwick in 1889. The team joined the Football League in 1892-93 and he then stepped down from the job. Furniss became a board member in 1903; he was later the club's chairman for a brief period, and he became the club's first president.

4. The first manager to win any league title with the club was Sam Ormerod, who guided it to the Second Division crown in 1898-99 and automatic promotion to the top flight. The former player and referee was appointed manager in August 1895 and held the title until July 1902. The side was relegated in 1901-02 and in debt and he felt it was the right time to resign. Ormerod went on to manage Stockport County and Clapton Orient before passing away in 1906.

5. When Man City hoisted the FA Cup for the first time in 1903-04, it was under the guidance of Tom Maley, an English-born player who spent his career in Scotland. Nicknamed "Handsome Tom," he managed City from July 1902 to July 1906, arriving just after the team was relegated to the Second Division. He earned promotion back to the First Division in his first season, though, by winning the league title. Maley then won the FA Cup and just missed a double as the team placed second in the league. However, City was accused of overpaying its players in 1905-06 and Maley was suspended for life by the Football Association, although the ban was lifted in July 1910. He then joined the Bradford Park Avenue club.

6. Wilf Wild took over as Man City boss from March 14, 1932, to December 1, 1946, making him the longest-serving manager in years. He was the first manager to win a First Division title, in 1936-37, and also added an FA Cup and FA Charity Shield to his collection. Wild had joined the club in 1920 as assistant secretary while others managed it. The team was relegated with Wild in charge and remained in the Second Division from 1939 to 1947, mainly due to World War II. However, he had left his position in 1946 after 14 years and Sam Cowan took over as manager. Wild was still Man City's secretary, though, when he passed away in 1950.

7. Joe Mercer was the boss from July 1965 to October 1971 and guided the squad to a First Division title, Second Division title, an FA Cup, and League Cup triumph as well as the European Cup Winners' Cup and an FA Charity Shield victory. After a successful playing career with Arsenal and Everton, Mercer managed Sheffield United and Aston Villa before arriving at Man City against the advice of his doctor. With Malcolm Allison as his assistant, City soon became one of the nation's most exciting teams. However, Allison took over as team manager while Mercer was made general manager and he left the club soon after.

8. In 1996-97, Man City played in the second-tier First Division after being relegated in 1995-96. It was a turbulent campaign that saw five different managers in charge of the squad. Three permanent bosses and a pair of

caretakers were appointed. Alan Ball was fired soon after the season kicked off with Asa Hartford taking over as caretaker. He was replaced by Steve Coppell, but Coppell resigned after just six games and 33 days because he claimed there was too much pressure on him. Phil Neal was appointed caretaker for the next 10 matches and after losing seven of them he was replaced by Frank Clark, who was still manager when the next season began.

9. Nicknamed "Mighty Mouse," Kevin Keegan was one of England's greatest players and later managed the national team as well as several top-flight clubs. One of these was Man City, as he was appointed in May 2001 and remained until March 2005. He led the team to the second-tier First Division title in 2001-02 after being relegated from the Premier League the season before. Once back in the top flight, Keegan's teams finished in 9th and 16th place in the next two campaigns. The side was promising in 2004-05 but Keegan agreed to leave his post on March 10, 2005, after admitting he wanted to retire at the end of the season. Stuart Pearce then took over as caretaker.

10. Pep Guardiola enjoyed tremendous success managing Barcelona and Bayern Munich by guiding those sides to over 21 major trophies, including a pair of European Champions League titles with Barcelona. Man City fans were thrilled when he arrived in 2016 and since then Guardiola has won another eight pieces of silverware: three League Cup, two Premier Leagues, one FA Cup championship, and a pair of FA Community Shields. He

also won the Premier League Manager of the Season award for 2017-18 and 2018-19. Guardiola was still managing the side in February 2021 and could easily have added more silverware by now.

CHAPTER 4:

GOALTENDING GREATS

QUIZ TIME!

1. How many matches did Shay Given play for the Irish national team?

    a. 97
    b. 112
    c. 134
    d. 142

2. Peter Schmeichel once scored a goal while playing with Man City.

    a. True
    b. False

3. Who was the keeper in Man City's first-ever Premier League match?

    a. Nicky Weaver
    b. Eike Immel
    c. Andy Dibble
    d. Tony Coton

4. Which keeper appeared in every match in the 2012-13 Premier League campaign?

    a. Costel Pantilimon
    b. Willy Caballero
    c. Joe Hart
    d. Richard Wright

5. Which keeper has made the most appearances in all competitions as of 2020?

    a. Charlie Williams
    b. Frank Swift
    c. Joe Corrigan
    d. Bert Trautmann

6. How many clean sheets did David James record in domestic league matches with Man City?

    a. 14
    b. 19
    c. 23
    d. 28

7. Frank Swift blamed his conceded goal in the 1933 FA Cup final on his decision not to wear gloves for the match.

    a. True
    b. False

8. With which club did Ederson record 32 clean sheets with before joining Man City?

    a. SL Benfica
    b. Rio Ave FC

c. GD Ribeirão

d. São Paulo FC

9. Who made 22 appearances in the 2016-17 Premier League?

a. Ederson

b. Costel Pantilimon

c. Claudio Bravo

d. Willy Caballero

10. How many clan sheets did Carlo Nash post in the 2001-02 First Division?

a. 2

b. 8

c. 10

d. 13

11. Which keeper kept 11 clean sheets in the 2004-05 domestic league?

a. Nicky Weaver

b. David Seaman

c. Kevin Stuhr-Ellegaard

d. David James

12. Ederson finished in second place for the Best FIFA Goalkeeper award in 2019.

a. True

b. False

13. How many times did Joe Hart win the Golden Glove award with Man City?

a. 7

b. 4

c. 6

d. 2

14. Which keeper helped Man City win its first FA Cup trophy?

    a. William Douglas

    b. Jim Goodchild

    c. Jack Hillman

    d. Charlie Williams

15. Which club did Joe Hart join Man City from?

    a. Blackpool FC

    b. Tranmere Rovers

    c. West Ham United

    d. Shrewsbury Town FC

16. Bert Trautmann was made an honorary officer of the Order of the British Empire.

    a. True

    b. False

17. How many appearances did Joe Corrigan make for Man City in all competitions?

    a. 492

    b. 595

    c. 603

    d. 621

18. Who made 15 appearances backing up Joe Hart in the 2008-09 Premier League?

    a. Shay Given
    b. Kasper Schmeichel
    c. Andreas Isaksson
    d. Márton Fülöp

19. How many times was Joe Hart capped by the English national team when he played for Man City?

    a. 64
    b. 27
    c. 50
    d. 35

20. Joe Corrigan won the FWA Footballer of the Year Award in 1968-69.

    a. True
    b. False

QUIZ ANSWERS

1. C – 134

2. B – False

3. D – Tony Coton

4. C – Joe Hart

5. C – Joe Corrigan

6. B – 19

7. A – True

8. A – SL Benfica

9. C – Claudio Bravo

10. C – 10

11. D – David James

12. B – False

13. B – 4

14. C – Jack Hillman

15. D – Shrewsbury Town FC

16. A – True

17. C – 603

18. A – Shay Given

19. A – 64

20. B – False

DID YOU KNOW?

1. Man City acquired Frank Swift in 1933 when first-choice keeper Len Langford was injured, and his replacement, James Nicholls, was struggling. Swift took over from Nicholls and allowed four goals on his debut but earned a clean sheet in his next match. He played in the 1936-37 FA Cup final against Portsmouth, which City won 2-1 and reportedly fainted at the final whistle due to emotion. Swift appeared in 375 games between 1933 and 1949 and became a sportswriter after retiring. Sadly, he was one of the victims of the infamous Munich air disaster in February 1958 when Manchester United's plane crashed.

2. Bert Trautmann was a Luftwaffe paratrooper during World War II and was held at a prisoner of war camp after being captured near the end of the conflict. After the war, he settled in England and played in goal for the local St. Helens club while working as a farmer. He joined Man City in 1949 and his signing was protested by many fans due to Trautmann's involvement in the recent war. However, his excellent performances soon silenced the critics, and he went on to appear in 545 matches with the club. He played in the 1954-1955 and 1955-1956 FA Cup finals, which resulted in a loss to Newcastle United followed by a win over Birmingham City. Trautmann was knocked unconscious against Birmingham and played the

remainder of the contest with a broken neck while making several remarkable saves.

3. Joe Corrigan joined Man City as a youth in 1966 and debuted for the first team a year later. He backed up Harry Dowd and didn't become a regular until 1969, though. Corrigan was a member of the side that hoisted both the League Cup and the European Cup Winners' Cup in 1969-1970 and he also helped capture the 1975-76 League Cup. He played nine times for England but, unfortunately, the timing wasn't right because Peter Shilton and Ray Clemence were the team's regular keepers. Corrigan played 603 games with City and was named the supporters' Player of the Year three times. He left to play in America in 1983.

4. Arriving at Maine Road in 1990 from Watford was Tony Coton, whose transfer fee was reportedly just shy of £1 million. He soon endeared himself to the fans with his superb performances and remained with the team until January 1996 when he moved across town to Manchester United for a reported £500,000. This at the time was a record fee between the two Manchester clubs. Coton was named the City Player of the Year for 1991-92 and 1993-94 and played almost 200 games with the team.

5. After spending 12 years, and appearing in 348 contests with Man City, Joe Hart moved on to Burnley in 2018. He joined City in 2006 from Shrewsbury Town, where he had played as a 17-year-old, and cost a reported £600,000 with

the fee rising to £1.5 million, depending on appearances. Hart posted a clean sheet on his debut but was sent out on loan several times during his City career. Hart helped the squad win the FA Cup in 2010-2011, the Premier League in 2011-2012 and 2013-2014, and the League Cup in 2013-2014 and 2015-16. He also played 75 times for England.

6. Shay Given of the Republic of Ireland was one of the country's and the Premier League's greatest keepers and joined Man City from Newcastle United in February 2009 for a reported £6 million. He posted over 115 clean sheets in 451 career league appearances with another in 52 in 134 outings as Ireland's most-capped keeper. In his final season with City, the club qualified for the European Champions League for the first time and won the FA Cup. However, Given played less than a handful of games that season and none in the league as Joe Hart took over as number one. After 69 appearances Given joined Aston Villa for a reported £3.5 million in July 2011.

7. English international David Seaman began his career before the Premier League was formed and played with several clubs before joining Man City from Arsenal in 2003 for his final season. His 142 clean sheets are among the most in league history and his 75 caps for England ranks second all-time for a goalie behind Peter Shilton. Seaman enjoyed his best years at Arsenal but joined City after the London side released him. He didn't play long, though, because he suffered an injury and, in January 2004, he announced he was retiring at the age of 40.

However, he helped manager Kevin Keegan choose his replacement and suggested fellow English international David James, who had knocked Seaman out of the number one job for England the previous year. Seaman did manage to appear in 26 games with City before hanging up his boots.

8. With 169 clean sheets in 572 career Premier League contests, David James ranks as one of the league's longest-serving and greatest keepers. The English international joined the club from West Ham United in January 2004 when David Seaman was injured and ready to retire. James played 17 games over the remainder of the season and all 38 league contests in each of the next two campaigns. In August 2006, he said he wanted to leave Manchester to be closer to his children in London and City sold James to Portsmouth for a reported £1.2 million.

9. Another all-time great who briefly played between the posts for Man City was "the Great Dane," Peter Schmeichel, who had made a name for himself with rival Manchester United for nine years. He had won numerous team and individual awards and was the first goalie to score in the league when he tallied for Aston Villa. Schmeichel's Premier League career ended in 2002-03 after joining from Villa on a free transfer. He played 29 league games and 31 in total. His draw and win over Manchester United meant he never lost a Manchester Derby game with either of the city's teams.

10. Brazilian international Ederson Santana de Moraes, simply known as "Ederson," joined Man City from Benfica in 2017 for a reported £35 million to become the world's most expensive goalkeeper at the time. He helped his teammates win the Premier League and League Cup in his first season and topped it the next campaign by winning the Premier League, FA Cup, and League Cup domestic treble. Ederson was named to the PFA Premier League Team of the Year in 2018-19 and won the league's Golden Glove in 2019-20 for the most "clean sheets" at 16. He was still with the team as of February 20201 and has won eight team trophies while closing in on 200 appearances.

CHAPTER 5:

DARING DEFENDERS

QUIZ TIME!

1. Which player made the most appearances for Man City?

    a. Stuart Pearce

    b. Mike Doyle

    c. Tommy Booth

    d. Paul Power

2. Micah Richards became the youngest defender for England's senior national team.

    a. True

    b. False

3. Who played 4,279 minutes in all competitions in 2010-11?

    a. Kolo Touré

    b. Pablo Zabaleta

    c. Joleon Lescott

    d. Vincent Kompany

4. How many times was Dave Watson capped by the English national team while playing for Man City?

    a. 51
    b. 48
    c. 30
    d. 22

5. Which player notched 3 goals in the 2018-19 Premier League?

    a. Danilo
    b. Vincent Kompany
    c. Aymeric Laporte
    d. Kyle Walker

6. Which defender was not shown 5 yellow cards in the 2002-03 Premier League?

    a. Sylvain Distin
    b. Jihai Sun
    c. Niclas Jensen
    d. Richard Dunne

7. Tony Book was the first player to win Man City's Player of the Year Award.

    a. True
    b. False

8. How many appearances did Tommy Booth make in all competitions for Man City?

    a. 386
    b. 473

c. 491

d. 512

9. What was Stuart Pearce's nickname?

   a. Psycho

   b. Big Cheese

   c. Slick Foot Stuart

   d. Passionate Pearce

10. Which defender scored 3 goals in the club's first Premier League season?

    a. Michael Vonk

    b. Keith Curle

    c. Terry Phelan

    d. Andy Hill

11. Paul Dickov was transferred to Man City by which club?

    a. Leicester City FC

    b. Brighton & Hove Albion FC

    c. Luton Town FC

    d. Arsenal FC

12. Tommy Booth was a co-winner of the FWA Footballer of the Year Award in 1968-69.

    a. True

    b. False

13. Who tallied 6 assists in all competitions in 2019-20?

    a. Kyle Walker

    b. Benjamin Mendy

c. Angeliño

d. João Cancelo

14. Who was the only player shown a red card in the 2002-03 Premier League?

    a. Sylvain Distin

    b. Danny Tiatto

    c. Jihai Sun

    d. Niclas Jensen

15. How many appearances did Mike Doyle make in all competitions with Man City?

    a. 468

    b. 517

    c. 570

    d. 582

16. Gaël Clichy was named to the FIFPro XI squad in 2012-13.

    a. True

    b. False

17. Which club did Aleksandar Kolarov play for when he was transferred to Man City?

    a. OFK Beogard

    b. S.S. Lazio

    c. FK Čukarički

    d. AS Roma

18. How many goals did Vincent Kompany score in all competitions for Man City?

a. 13

b. 25

c. 16

d. 20

19. Nicolás Otamendi was a member of which squad before joining Man City?

    a. CA Vélez Sarsfield

    b. CA Mineiro

    c. Valencia CF

    d. FC Porto

20. Richard Dunne was shown 2 red cards in all competitions in 2008-09.

    a. True

    b. False

QUIZ ANSWERS

1. B – Mike Doyle

2. A – True

3. D – Vincent Kompany

4. C – 30

5. C – Aymeric Laporte

6. B – Jihai Sun

7. A – True

8. C – 491

9. A – Psycho

10. B – Keith Curle

11. D – Arsenal FC

12. A – True

13. A – Kyle Walker

14. B – Danny Tiatto

15. C – 570

16. B – False

17. B – S.S. Lazio

18. D – 20

19. C – Valencia CF

20. A – True

DID YOU KNOW?

1. English international defender Stuart Pearce was one of Man City's toughest defenders. Nicknamed "Psycho,"' he was fair but firm and regularly played through pain. He also possessed plenty of skill and a thunderous shot that resulted in over 100 goals during his career. The tough-tackling left-back played with City for just one season at the end of his career in 2001-02. He captained the squad to the First Division title, scoring on a direct free kick on his debut. After hanging up his boots, he remained with the club as a coach and later became City's manager.

2. At one time, Micah Richards was considered one of England's best defenders. He kicked off his career with Man City and made nearly 250 appearances between 2005 and 2014. He was then sent on loan to Fiorentina in Italy for a season and signed with Aston Villa in June 2015. The English international won the FA Cup with City in 2010-11 and the Premier League title the next year. When he made his England debut in November 2006, he became the team's youngest defender ever, as he had turned 18 just a few months earlier. Richards retired in 2019 and later returned to City as a club ambassador.

3. Welsh international David 'Di" Jones began his career in 1882 and was well known for his two-footed play, versatility, and strong tackling. He captained Bolton

Wanderers at the 1894 FA Cup final and signed with Man City in 1898, where he joined former teammate Billy Meredith. Jones helped the club win the Second Division in his first season and promotion to the top flight. On Aug. 17, 1902, after appearing in 118 games for the team, Jones was playing in a pre-season friendly when he fell to the ground and cut his knee on a piece of glass. The cut became infected, and Jones passed away from blood poisoning and lockjaw 10 days later.

4. Argentine international Pablo Zabaleta was a tenacious defender who joined Man City in 2008 from Espanyol after turning down offers from Juventus. He won all of the major trophies available in England with City over the next nine years before leaving for West Ham United in 2017. After 333 appearances and a dozen goals, Zabaleta left town with two Premier League titles under his belt along with an FA Cup, two League Cups, and an FA Community Shield triumph. He was named to the PFA Premier League Team of the Year for 2012-13.

5. Serbian international Aleksandar Kolarov Joined Man City from Lazio in 2010 for a reported fee of £16 million. Kolarov was comfortable playing anywhere in the back four but was famous for his overlapping attacking runs down the left wing. He played close to 250 games and chipped in with over 20 goals and 35 assists. He also helped the side capture two Premier League championships, an FA Cup, two League Cups, and an FA

Community Shield. Zabaleta, who was named the Serbian Player of the Year for 2011, joined Roma in 2017.

6. Sylvain Distin was a French defender who was sent on loan to Newcastle United from Paris Saint-Germain in 2001-02 but turned down the chance of joining the English side permanently. He was then sold to Man City for a reported £4 million, setting a club record for a defender at the time. Distin played over 200 times with the team with just over a handful of goals to his name before joining Portsmouth in 2007. He was named the team's Player of the Year in his first season and was handed the captain's armband before the 2003-04 kickoff.

7. Another French defender who stood out at the club was international Gaël Clichy, who arrived from Arsenal in 2011 for an undisclosed fee that was reported to be approximately £7 million. He soon became the side's first choice left-back, starting as a backup for Aleksandar Kolarov. Clichy played in just over 200 matches with Man City while helping the squad capture the Premier League in 2011-12 and 2013-14, as well as the League Cup in 2013-14 and 2015-16 and the 2012 FA Community Shield. Clichy then left for İstanbul Başakşehir in May 2017.

8. Jesús Navas was a Spanish international who excelled at right-back and could also play on the wing. He had already played a decade with Sevilla before arriving at Man City in June 2013 for a reported £14.9 million. He spent four seasons in England before returning to Sevilla

in 2017. In between, he played just under 200 games with the team and contributed eight goals and 39 assists. His inspired play also helped the side capture the Premier League crown in 2013-14 and the League Cup in 2013-14 and 2015-16.

9. When Keith Curle joined Man City from Wimbledon in 1991, he cost £2.5 million, which was reportedly a club record at the time. Curle eventually wore the captain's armband with the team and would go on to play just over 200 games and post 13 goals. City finished in fifth place in Curle's first season, and his play earned him a call up to England's national side. He was part of the Euro 92 squad. City was relegated from the Premier League in 1995-96 and Curle lost the captaincy. He was then sold to the Wolverhampton Wanderers for a reported £650,000 in August 1996.

10. Chinese international Sun Jihai was transferred from Dalian Shide in his homeland to Man City in 2002 for a reported £2 million and he became City's first Asian-born player. He soon became a cult hero due to his solid defending and dangerous attacking skills. In October 2002, he became the first East Asian to score in the Premier League and then became the first Chinese player to tally in the UEFA Cup. Sun played 151 games and helped City hoist the second-tier First Division trophy in 2001-02. He joined Sheffield United in 2008 and returned to China in 2009, where he's now a multi-millionaire tech mogul.

CHAPTER 6:

MAESTROS OF THE MIDFIELD

QUIZ TIME!

1. Who holds the record for most appearances in all competitions for Man City as of 2020?

   a. Asa Hartford
   b. Ian Brightwell
   c. Alan Oakes
   d. Colin Bell

2. Kevin De Bruyne was named to the FIFPro XI squad for the first time in 2020.

   a. True
   b. False

3. Which club was Yaya Touré playing for before he signed with Man City?

   a. AS Monaco
   b. FC Barcelona
   c. Olympiacos Piraeus
   d. K.S.K. Beveren

4. Which player netted 5 goals in the club's inaugural Premier League season?

   a. Fitzroy Simpson
   b. Michael Vonk
   c. Rick Holden
   d. Gary Flitcroft

5. How many times was Collin Bell capped by the English national team?

   a. 27
   b. 33
   c. 48
   d. 55

6. Which player was shown 9 yellow cards in the 2004-05 domestic league?

   a. Lee Croft
   b. Willo Flood
   c. Paul Bosvelt
   d. Joey Barton

7. Kevin De Bruyne earned 25 assists in all competitions in 2016-17.

   a. True
   b. False

8. Which player scored 6 goals in the 2008-09 Premier League?

   a. Elano
   b. Gelson Fernandes

c. Dietmar Hamann

d. Michael Johnson

9. Which club did Gareth Barry leave to join Man City?

    a. Leeds United

    b. Nottingham Forest

    c. Aston Villa

    d. Everton FC

10. How many goals did Fernandinho score in the 2017-18 domestic league?

    a. 5

    b. 7

    c. 3

    d. 10

11. Which player appeared in 35 Premier League matches in the 2000-01 season?

    a. Tony Grant

    b. Jeff Whitely

    c. Kevin Horlock

    d. Alf-Inge Håland

12. After Alan Oakes left Man City, he signed with rival Manchester United.

    a. True

    b. False

13. How many official appearances did Alan Oakes make in all competitions for Man City?

a. 704

b. 680

c. 635

d. 583

14. Kevin De Bruyne left which club to join Man City?

   a. KRC Genk

   b. Werder Bremen

   c. VfL Wolfsburg

   d. Chelsea FC

15. How many appearances did James Milner make for the English national team while playing for Man City?

   a. 51

   b. 42

   c. 36

   d. 25

16. Fabian Delph was the only player on Man City to be shown a red card in all competitions in 2017-18.

   a. True

   b. False

17. How many appearances did Colin Bell make for the club in all competitions?

   a. 331

   b. 342

   c. 488

   d. 501

18. Which player appeared in 49 matches in all competitions in 2013-14?

    a. Javi García

    b. James Milner

    c. Fernandinho

    d. Yaya Touré

19. Which club did Shaun Wright-Phillips join after his first stint with Man City?

    a. New York Red Bulls

    b. Queens Park Rangers

    c. Chelsea FC

    d. Fulham FC

20. Yaya Touré won the FWA Footballer of the Year Award in 2016.

    a. True

    b. False

QUIZ ANSWERS

1. C – Alan Oakes

2. A – True

3. B – FC Barcelona

4. D – Garry Flitcroft

5. C – 48

6. D – Joey Barton

7. B – False

8. A – Elano

9. C – Aston Villa

10. A – 5

11. D – Alf-Inge Håland

12. B – False

13. B – 680

14. C – VfL Wolfsburg

15. B – 42

16. A – True

17. D – 501

18. D – Yaya Touré

19. C – Chelsea FC

20. B – False

DID YOU KNOW?

1. After starring at the 2017 Under-17 World Cup, where he won the Golden Ball as the tournament's best player, it was obvious Phil Foden had what it takes to succeed. He possesses tremendous playmaking, dribbling, and scoring skills, even though he's just 5-feet, 7-inches tall. Foden has been with Man City since he was nine years old and as of February 2021, had played over 100 games and scored more than 25 goals. He's also won eight trophies with the side and became the youngest owner of a Premier League winners' medal and the team's youngest scorer in the European Champions League.

2. Portuguese international Bernardo Silva is a fine playmaker and world-class midfielder who joined Man City from Monaco in 2017 for a reported fee of £43.5 million. He helped the side win the Premier League and League Cup in his first season and the domestic triple the next campaign when he hoisted the FA Cup, League Cup, and league title. Silva was also recognized individually by being named the club's 2019 Player of the Year and he made the PFA Premier League Team of the Year. As of February 2021, he had eight winners' medals and had netted 34 goals in 184 outings.

3. Georgian international Georgi Kinkladze arrived at Man City from Dinamo Tbilisi in his homeland in 1995 where

his spine-tingling goals and dribbling ability made him a cult hero. He was named the club's Player of the Year for 1996 and 1997 and remained loyal to the side after it was relegated to the second-tier First Division in 1996. However, when City was relegated again in 1998, he joined Dutch champions Ajax. Kinkladze netted 22 goals in 121 games and his entertaining and dazzling play was one of the club's bright spots in one of its leanest periods.

4. Shaun Wright-Phillips is the adopted son of former Arsenal legend Ian Wright and the brother of Bradley Wright-Phillips, the current all-time leading scorer for his former team the New York Red Bulls. The 5-foot, 5-inch Shaun played with Man City from 1999 to 2005 before joining Chelsea. He then returned from 2008 to 2011 and played just over 270 matches, scoring 48 goals. The English international was one of the world's fastest players and also possesses a lethal shot. Wright-Phillips was the team's Player of the Year in 2004 and won the 2010-11 FA Cup. He was also the side's Young Player of the Year four seasons in a row, from 1999-2000 through 2002-03, and made the PFA Premier Team of the Year in 2004-05.

5. With 680 official appearances to his name, Alan Oakes holds the Man City record for games played. He joined in 1958, turned pro a year later as a teenager, and remained until leaving for Chester in 1976. City was relegated in 1963-64 and Oakes helped win the Second Division two years later to return to the top flight. The team won the league in 1967-68, the FA Cup in 1968-69, the European

Cup Winners' Cup in 1969-70, and a pair of League Cups and FA Charity Shields with Oakes' help. He was the club's Player of the Year in 1975.

6. Ivory Coast international Yaya Touré, the brother and Man City teammate of Kolo Touré, excelled as a box-to-box midfielder during his career. He joined in 2010 from Barcelona and displayed superb defensive and offensive abilities. He notched 24 goals in 2013-14, with 20 of them coming in the Premier League, where the team won the championship9. Touré helped the side capture three league titles, two League Cups, and an FA Cup and FA Community Shield. He was the club's Player of the Year for 2013-14 and twice made the PFA Premier League Team of the Year. He was also named African Footballer of the Year four straight times, from 2011 through 2014.

7. When it comes to creativity, great technique, and the ability to score, Spanish international David Silva was second to none. He spent a decade with Man City after joining in 2010 from Valencia and before leaving for Real Sociedad in 2020. As well as winning numerous individual awards, he helped the side win the Premier League in 2020-11 and added three more league crowns, five League Cups, two FA Cups, and three FA Community Shields. Silva played just over 430 games and netted 77 goals and over 100 assists. the club is planning to erect a statue of him outside Etihad Stadium.

8. Nicky Summerbee played with several clubs during his pro career but is best known for his stint with Man City.

He joined from Swindon Town in 1994 and left in 1997 for Sunderland. Summerbee was under a lot of pressure at Maine Road because his father, Mike Summerbee, was a Man City cult legend and his grandfather, George Summerbee, and great uncle, Gordon Summerbee, were also pro soccer players. Nicky played 156 games with the team before moving on and later won the First Division title with Sunderland. He became a well-known broadcasting pundit after retiring.

9. German international Leroy Sané left Schalke 04 for Man City in 2014 for a reported initial fee of £37 million fee. He quickly fit in and was named the PFA Young Player of the Year for the Premier League in 2017-18 after helping the team win both the league and the League Cup. The side won both again the next season, along with the FA Cup, for an unprecedented domestic treble. Sané helped the team win seven trophies and notched nearly 40 goals in 134 matches before being dispatched to Bayern Munich for a City club-record fee of a reported £45 million.

10. Attacking midfielder Samir Nasri was a French international known for his dribbling, passing, and ball control. After establishing himself at Marseille, he joined Arsenal in 2008 and was named the French Player of the Year 2010. He signed with Man City in August 2011 and won the Premier League title in his first campaign. Nasri then helped the team win the league and League Cup double in 2013-14 and the 2012 FA Community Shield. He was named to the PFA Premier League Team of the Year

for 2010-11. He was loaned to Sevilla in 2016-17 and then signed for Turkish club Antalyaspor in August 2017 after netting 27 goals in 176 outings for City.

CHAPTER 7:

SENSATIONAL STRIKERS/FORWARDS

QUIZ TIME!

1. Which player appeared in more games for the club?

    a. Billy Meredith

    b. Neil Young

    c. Eric Brook

    d. Mike Summerbee

2. Sergio Agüero tallied 10 assists in the 2016-17 Premier League.

    a. True

    b. False

3. Who scored 10 goals in all competitions in 2010-11?

    a. Mario Balotelli

    b. David Silva

    c. Edin Džeko

    d. Adam Johnson

4. Gabriel Jesus won the player of the year award with which Brazilian club before joining Man City?

    a. São Paulo FC
    b. EC Água Santa
    c. Ituano FC
    d. SE Palmeiras

5. How many goals did Sergio Agüero tally in all competitions in 2014-15?

    a. 35
    b. 27
    c. 40
    d. 32

6. David Silva played for which club before joining Man City?

    a. Cádiz CF
    b. SD Eibar
    c. Valencia CF
    d. Celta de Vigo

7. Billy Meredith played for Manchester United before joining Man City.

    a. True
    b. False

8. Uwe Rösler was playing for which club before he was loaned to Man City?

    a. 1. FC Nürnberg
    b. SG Dynamo Dresden

c. 1.FC Magdeburg

d. BSG Chemie Leipzig

9. Who won the FWA Footballer of the Year Award in 2018-19?

a. Raheem Sterling

b. Gabriel Jesus

c. Leroy Sané

d. David Silva

10. How many goals did Darius Vassell score in the 2007-08 domestic league?

a. 13

b. 10

c. 6

d. 4

11. How many appearances did Billy Meredith make for Man City in all competitions?

a. 416

b. 394

c. 360

d. 275

12. David Silva holds the club record for most assists in all competitions with 143.

a. True

b. False

13. How many goals did Francis Lee score for the English national team?

a. 5

b. 7

c. 10

d. 15

14. Which player scored 10 goals in the 2017-18 Premier League?

    a. Jack Harrison

    b. David Silva

    c. Brahim Díaz

    d. Leroy Sané

15. How many appearances did Eric Brook make for the team in all competitions?

    a. 378

    b. 426

    c. 494

    d. 541

16. Nicolas Anelka played in every match in the 2002-03 domestic league season.

    a. True

    b. False

17. Which player scored 5 goals in the 1993-94 Premier League?

    a. Carl Griffiths

    b. Niall Quinn

    c. Paul Walsh

    d. David Rocastle

18. Who tallied 14 goals in the 2011-12 Premier League season?

    a. Eden Džeko
    b. Mario Balotelli
    c. Adam Johnson
    d. Carlos Tevez

19. How many assists did Samir Nasri earn in the 2013-14 Premier League?

    a. 5
    b. 7
    c. 9
    d. 11

20. Sergio Agüero has been named to the FIFPro XI squad twice as of 2020.

    a. True
    b. False

QUIZ ANSWERS

1. C – Eric Brook

2. B – False

3. A – Mario Balotelli

4. D – SE Palmeiras

5. D – 32

6. C – Valencia CF

7. B – False

8. A – 1. FC Nürnberg

9. A – Raheem Sterling

10. C – 6

11. B – 394

12. B – False

13. C – 10

14. D – Leroy Sané

15. C – 494

16. A – True

17. B – Niall Quinn

18. A – Eden Džeko

19. C – 9

20. B – False

DID YOU KNOW?

1. Mike Summerbee found more success with the club than his son, as he helped the team win seven pieces of silverware. The England international joined in 1965 from Swindon Town, where he played as a 16-year-old, and left for Burnley a decade later. Nicknamed "Buzzer," Summerbee was known as one of the "Holy Trinity" at City, along with Francis Lee and Colin Bell. He played 452 times and chipped in with 67 goals. He was the club's Player of the Year in 1972 and 1973 and was inducted into the Manchester City FC Hall of Fame. Summerbee also starred in the cult film *Escape to Victory* with Sylvester Stallone, Michael Caine, and Pelé.

2. Brazilian international Gabriel Jesus is currently starring with Man City after joining from Palmeiras in his home nation in January 2017 for a reported £27 million plus add-ons. Jesus won a gold medal at the 2016 Olympics and is known for his fine finishing touch. He became the first City player to notch a goal and assist in his first Premier League start. Jesus has helped the side win three League Cups, two Premier League titles, an FA Cup, and two FA Community Shields. He's suffered a few injuries with the squad but had tallied 77 goals in 178 outings as of February 2021.

3. With 108 goals in 416 games, Neil Young may not have scored the most goals for his hometown team, but he

netted some of the most important. He joined as a youth player and appeared with the senior side from 1961 to 1972 before signing with Preston North End. Young scored the lone goal of the game in the 1968-1969 FA Cup final and also found the back of the net in the 1969-1970 European Cup Winners' Cup final, which the team also won. Young also won a First Division title, Second Division title, and FA Charity Shield with the side.

4. Shaun Goater led the club in scoring for four straight seasons after joining from Bristol City in 1998 and, with 32 goals in 37 games for the Bermuda national team, he was a natural-born scorer. He posted 103 goals in 210 appearances for City and one of them came nine seconds after entering a game as a substitute to set a Premier League record. He helped the team win the third-tier Second Division playoffs in 1998-99 and the second-tier First Division title in 2001-02. He won the First Division Golden Boot in 2001-02 and was named to the PFA Team of the Year in 1997-98 and 2001-02. Goater was the club's Player of the Year for 2000. Fans created a song called "Feed the Goat and He Will Score" for him.

5. Republic of Ireland international Niall Quinn had great height for a striker at 6-feet, 4-inches, which helped the 1991 Man City Player of the Year notch 78 goals in 243 contests. He joined for a reported £800,000 from Arsenal in March 1990, scored in his debut, and remained until finishing his career with a highly successful spell at Sunderland for a club-record £1.3 million for the northeast

team. In a 1991, 2-1 victory over Derby County, Quinn scored and then saved a penalty kick as he filled in between the posts after goalkeeper Tony Coton had been sent off.

6. Center-forward Uwe Rösler of East Germany arrived at Man City on a trial basis in March 1994 from FC Nürnberg and earned a spot on the team after scoring twice against Burnley in his first outing. He was bought for a fee of £500,000 and remained at the club for four years while leading the side in scoring for three straight seasons. He tallied 64 goals in 176 matches and was the team's Player of the Year for 1995. Rösler helped the side avoid relegation during his first season and the club's fans adopted a Pet Shop Boys song named "Go West" to chant Rösler's name from the Maine Road terraces. He left for Kaiserslautern in 1998 and the member of the club's hall of fame became a football manager after retiring.

7. After arriving from Queens Park Rangers for what was then a Man City record £200,000 in 1972, Rodney Marsh went on to contribute 47 goals in 152 outings. He led the side with 19 goals in his first campaign and dazzled the fans with his dribbling expertise and showmanship. The English international helped the team reach the 1973-74 League Cup final and won the 1972 FA Charity Shield with the side. Marsh left to play in America in 1976 and later became a manager and media pundit. Roger Daltrey, lead singer of rock band The Who, portrayed Marsh in a 2000 movie about George Best, and Marsh is featured on

the cover of the album "Definitely Maybe" by rock band Oasis.

8. English international Dennis Tueart signed for Man City in 1974 from Sunderland for what was then a club record £275,000. He helped the squad capture the 1976 League Cup by scoring the winning goal with a spectacular overhead kick. That was one of the 109 he tallied for the team in 275 appearances, which came with two stints. He left in 1978 to play in America with the New York Cosmos and scored twice in the league's cup final to win the 1978 Soccer Bowl. Tueart rejoined Man City in February 1980 until the club was relegated in 1982-83 when he joined Stoke City. He later became a director at Man City until 2007 after a 33-year association with the club.

9. Another player who enjoyed two spells with Man City was English international winger Peter Barnes, who notched 22 goals in 151 games with the side. He is also one of the few players who suited up with both of his hometown clubs, Manchester United and City. Barnes kicked off his career with City from 1974 to 1979 and was named the PFA Young Player of the Year after scoring in the 1975-1976 League Cup final win over Newcastle United when he was 18 years old. He was sold to West Bromwich Albion for that club's record fee of £748,000. Barnes returned from Man United for the 1987-88 campaign but was sent out on loan for most of the season.

10. Don Revie may be best known as manager and player with Leeds United and England, but he appeared in more

games with Man City than anybody else. He joined in 1951 from Hull City and departed for Sunderland in 1956. He played 178 games with the club and chipped in with 41 goals. Revie's side reached the 1954-55 FA Cup final but fell 3-1 to Newcastle United. In 1955-56, he was suspended for two weeks after falling out with manager Les McDowall but still played in that season's FA Cup final, which Man City won 3-1 over Birmingham City. Revie was sold to Sunderland a few months later. In 1954-1955, Revie became the first City player to be named the Football Writers' Player of the Year.

CHAPTER 8:

NOTABLE TRANSFERS/SIGNINGS

QUIZ TIME!

1. Who is the club's most expensive signing as of 2020?

    a. Kevin De Bruyne

    b. Rúben Dias

    c. Rodri

    d. Riyad Mahrez

2. Man City did not pay a transfer fee for any of their signings in 2006-07.

    a. True

    b. False

3. Who was the club's most expensive signing in 2008-09?

    a. Nigel de Jong

    b. Carlos Tevez

    c. Robinho

    d. Jô

4. How much did Man City reportedly pay Atlético Madrid to acquire Sergio Agüero?

   a. €48 million
   b. €40 million
   c. €32 million
   d. €23 million

5. Man City signed Raheem Sterling from which team in 2015-16?

   a. Queens Park Rangers
   b. Arsenal FC
   c. Brighton & Hove Albion FC
   d. Liverpool FC

6. Who was the most expensive player Man City has sold as of 2020?

   a. Danilo
   b. Leroy Sané
   c. Shaun Wright-Phillips
   d. Robinho

7. Man City received a transfer fee of approximately €20 million from AC Milan for Mario Balotelli.

   a. True
   b. False

8. Man City paid a reported €24 million for which player, who went on to make just 42 appearances in all competitions?

   a. Scott Sinclair
   b. Emanuel Adebayor

c. Jô

d. Wilfrid Bony

9. How much did Man City reportedly pay to acquire Rúben Dias?

   a. €44 million

   b. €49 million

   c. €55 million

   d. €68 million

10. Which club did Man City sell Danilo to in 2019-20?

    a. S.S.C. Napoli

    b. Borussia Dortmund

    c. FC Barcelona

    d. Juventus

11. Man City transferred Shaun Wright-Phillips to which outfit, for a reported €31 million?

    a. Chelsea FC

    b. Manchester United

    c. S.S. Lazio

    d. Atalanta BC

12. Man City received a transfer fee of €55 million when the club transferred Leroy Sané.

    a. True

    b. False

13. Which player was the club's most expensive signing in 2017-18?

a. Kyle Walker

b. Ederson

c. Benjamin Mendy

d. Aymeric Laporte

14. From which team did Man City acquire Riyad Mahrez in 2018-19?

    a. Quimper Kerfeunteun FC

    b. AAS Sarcelles

    c. Leicester City

    d. AC Le Havre

15. How much did the club reportedly pay to acquire Kevin De Bruyne?

    a. €43 million

    b. €65 million

    c. €76 million

    d. €80 million

16. Man City paid over €11 million for Fabian Delph, who appeared in just 89 matches in all competitions with the squad

    a. True

    b. False

17. To which side did Man City transfer Leroy Sané in 2020-21?

    a. Inter Milan

    b. Paris Saint-Germain

    c. Real Madrid

    d. Bayern Munich

18. The club spent a reported €37 million on what player in 2010-11?

    a. Yaya Touré
    b. Edin Džeko
    c. David Silva
    d. Aleksandar Kolarov

19. How much did Man City reportedly pay to acquire Joe Hart from Shrewsbury Town?

    a. €50 thousand
    b. €900 thousand
    c. €5 million
    d. €8 million

20. The club sold Riyad Mahrez to Liverpool in the 2021 January transfer window.

    a. True
    b. False

QUIZ ANSWERS

1. A – Kevin De Bruyne

2. B – False

3. C - Robinho

4. B – €40 million

5. D – Liverpool FC

6. B – Leroy Sané

7. A – True

8. C – Jô

9. D – €68 million

10. D – Juventus

11. A – Chelsea FC

12. B – False

13. D – Aymeric Laporte

14. C – Leicester City

15. B – €76 million

16. A – True

17. D – Bayern Munich

18. B – Edin Džeko

19. B – €900 thousand

20. B – False

DID YOU KNOW?

1. As of February 2021, the five highest transfer fees paid by Man City in club history are midfielder Kevin De Bruyne from VfL Wolfsburg for £68.4 million in 2015-16; defender Rúben Dias from SL Benfica for £61.2 million in 2020-21; winger Riyad Mahrez from Leicester City for £61.02 million in 2018-19; defender João Cancelo from Juventus FC for £58.5 million in 2019-20; and defender Aymeric Laporte from Athletic Bilbao for £58.5 million in 2017-18.

2. As of February 2021, the five highest transfer fees received by Man City in club history are winger Leroy Sané to Bayern Munich for £40.5 million in 2020-21; defender Danilo to Juventus FC for £33.3 million in 2019-20; winger Shaun Wright-Phillips to Chelsea FC for £28.35 million in 2005-06; forward Álvaro Negredo to Valencia CF for £25.2 million in 2016-15; and forward Kelechi Iheanacho to Leicester City for £24.93 million in 2017-18.

3. Man City manager Mark Hughes forked over what was then a club-record £21.6 million to CSKA Moscow for striker João Alves de Assis Silva, otherwise known as Jô. In return, the club received 1 league goal and 6 in all 42 games in all competitions. This was quite a shock, considering Jô tallied 44 goals in 77 outings with Moscow. City loaned the player to Everton by early 2009 and then to Turkish club Galatasaray after Everton had suspended

him for flying home to Brazil without permission at Christmas. Jô was handed a lifeline with City in 2010-11 but repaid their faith with just 3 goals in 23 matches. He then headed back to Brazil to play in July 2011 on a free transfer.

4. Argentine international striker Carlos Tevez crossed from the red side of Manchester to the blue side in 2009 when Man City acquired him from Manchester United for a reported £26.1 million. Tevez was apparently insulted by a contract offer from United manager Sir Alex Ferguson and was unhappy about his lack of playing time. Tevez was on loan with United from West Ham at the time. United had offered West Ham £25.5 million for him in a permanent deal and Tevez was offered a five-year contract but turned it down. After joining City, Tevez refused to come on as a substitute in a European Champions League match in September 2011. He was suspended and fined by the club, which tried to sell him. No takers were found and, after Tevez apologized publicly, he was allowed to rejoin the squad after an absence of several months.

5. English international winger Raheem Sterling joined Man City in 2015-16 from Liverpool for a reported £57.33 million to set a record for an English player. Sterling publicly announced he wanted to leave Anfield even though he was under contract at £35,000 a week for two more years. Things turned nasty when Liverpool rejected several bids and Sterling denounced manager Brendan Rodgers in the media. Sterling claimed money had nothing

to do with the saga even though City was prepared to pay him £200,000 a week compared to Liverpool's offer of £100,000. He threatened to skip Liverpool's pre-season tour of Asia and Australia and was then sold.

6. Defender Joleon Lescott was one of Everton's most consistent performers and the club rejected bids for its two-time player of the year in 2009. Lescott knew Man City was interested in him now and handed Everton an official transfer request which manager David Moyes rejected. Lescott then claimed he didn't want to play in Everton's 2009-10 opening match, but he was named in the squad anyway. Moyes dropped him a week later, citing his attitude as the reason. The manager folded shortly after and sold Lescott to City for a reported £24.75 million. Lescott played just over 100 league games and was released for nothing in 2014.

7. Aston Villa skipper Fabian Delph repeatedly assured the club and its fans that he would remain at Villa Park for the 2015-16 campaign. He stated that he was loyal to the side and didn't want to leave, even though Man City had agreed to pay the £8 million release clause in his contract. Villa was pleased by his loyalty and wanted to raise his weekly wages from £50,000 to £80,000 per week as a reward. Just a week later, Delph decided to join City after they offered him £100,000 a week. Villa fans predictably went ballistic on social media platforms, while Delph's City career lasted just 57 league games over four seasons before he was sold to Everton.

8. Man City bought Aymeric Laporte from Athletic Bilbao in January 2018 for £58.5 million to set what was then a record fee for both clubs. The French center-back appeared in nine league games while City won the Premier League with 100 points, meaning he was eligible for a winners' medal. In 2019-20, he played 51 games in all competitions to help the club win the first domestic treble in English history by capturing the Premier League, FA Cup, and League Cup. The side also won the FA Community Shield as a bonus. However, in August 2019, he suffered a knee injury and underwent surgery that limited him to 20 appearances. Laporte was back at his usual spot in 2020-21, though.

9. Portuguese international center-back Rúben Dias was acquired by Man City on Sept. 29, 2020, for £61.2 million and reportedly signed a six-year contract. In addition, Man City sold Argentine defender Nicolás Otamendi to Benfica as part of the transaction. Otamendi had spent five seasons with the club and appeared in over 200 games. He also helped the side win nine trophies and was named to the PFA Premier League Team of the Year for 2017-18. Meanwhile, the 23-year-old Dias was named City's Player of the Month for November 2020 due to his strong defensive performances and could have a long future at the club.

10. Belgian international Kevin De Bruyne is Man City's most expensive signing so far, costing £68.4 million from VfL Wolfsburg in August 2015. He's been worth the money as

De Bruyne is generally considered to be one of the most complete players and midfielders in the world due to his playmaking and scoring skills. He's played just over 250 games with the squad as of February 2021 and chipped in with 60 goals. He's also won nine team trophies already and numerous individual awards, including being named the Premier League Player of the Season and PFA Players' Player of the Year for 2019-20.

CHAPTER 9:

ODDS & ENDS

QUIZ TIME!

1. Which is not one of Man City's nicknames?

    a. The Boats
    b. The Sky Blues
    c. The Citizens
    d. Cityzens

2. Man City shared Maine Road Stadium with Manchester United for a few years after Old Trafford was damaged in World War II.

    a. True
    b. False

3. Man City's biggest win in the Premier League as of 2020 was 8-0 against which club?

    a. Burton Albion FC
    b. Watford FC
    c. Preston North End
    d. Birmingham City FC

4. How many matches did the club win in its only season in the Football Alliance?

    a. 10

    b. 7

    c. 6

    d. 4

5. Who was the youngest player to make an appearance for Man City at 15 years and 314 days old?

    a. Paul Simpson

    b. Glyn Pardoe

    c. Karim Rekik

    d. Brahim Díaz

6. Man City's biggest victory in a European match was against which side in the 2018-19 UEFA Champions League?

    a. AEK Athens

    b. CSKA Moscow

    c. FC Schalke 04

    d. Shakhtar Donetsk

7. Matches between Man City and Manchester United are referred to as the "Manchester Derby."

    a. True

    b. False

8. Man City scored 11 goals in a blowout victory against which club in an 1895 league outing?

    a. Newton Heath

    b. Grimsby Town FC

c. Woolwich Arsenal

d. Lincoln City FC

9. How many games did the side win in its first season in the Premier League?

a. 10

b. 12

c. 15

d. 20

10. Who was the first Man City player to win the Premier League Player of the Month award?

a. Carlos Tevez

b. Micah Richards

c. David Silva

d. Edin Džeko

11. Who was the oldest player to make an appearance for the team at 49 years and 245 days?

a. Stuart Pearce

b. David Seaman

c. John Burridge

d. Billy Meredith

12. Between Aug. 26 and Dec. 27, 2017, Man City went on an 18-game Premier League winning streak.

a. True

b. False

13. Who is the only player to have won the FIFA World Cup while playing for Man City?

a. Billy Meredith

b. Benjamin Mendy

c. David Silva

d. Matt Busby

14. The club's record defeat in a Premier League match as of 2020 was 8-1 to which club?

a. Swansea City

b. Manchester United

c. Burton Wanderers

d. Middlesbrough FC

15. What is the most goals the club scored in a single domestic league season as of 2020?

a. 87

b. 102

c. 99

d. 108

16. Kevin De Bruyne has won the Premier League Playmaker of the Season award twice as of 2020.

a. True

b. False

17. The team's record for biggest victory in a League Cup match is 9-0 against which side in 2019?

a. Oxford United

b. Burton Albion FC

c. Leicester City FC

d. Fulham FC

18. How many games did Man City lose in 2005-06 to set a club record for most losses in a Premier League campaign?

    a. 16
    b. 19
    c. 21
    d. 23

19. How many domestic league games did Man City draw in 1993-94?

    a. 11
    b. 15
    c. 18
    d. 20

20. David Silva was capped by the Spanish national team 87 times while was playing for Man City.

    a. True
    b. False

QUIZ ANSWERS

1. A – The Boats

2. A – True

3. B – Watford FC

4. C – 6

5. B – Glyn Pardoe

6. C – FC Schalke 04

7. A – True

8. D – Lincoln City FC

9. C – 15

10. B – Micah Richards

11. D – Billy Meredith

12. A – True

13. B – Benjamin Mendy

14. D – Middlesbrough FC

15. D – 108

16. A – True

17. B – Burton Albion FC

18. C – 21

19. C – 18

20. A – True

DID YOU KNOW?

1. Manchester City was founded when two church wardens attempted to derail alcoholism and local gang violence in the Gorton area of Manchester. They instituted new activities for local men who were typically unemployed at the time. All men were welcomed to join the club regardless of religion.

2. In 1905-06, the club was alleged of committing financial irregularities and overpaying players. A total of 17 players were then suspended in 1906, along with a director and the manager. Club captain Billy Meredith was one of those banned and he then moved across town to join Manchester United.

3. The Hyde Road stadium in West Gorton, Manchester, was built in 1887 and was used by Man City until 1923. Before being developed into a soccer ground, the site was simply a wasteland. The first stand was erected in 1888 and the venue had no change rooms until 1896. Before that, players changed in a nearby pub called the Hyde Road Hotel. However, by 1904 the stadium could hold 40,000 fans.

4. The Hyde Road ground suffered fire damage to its main stand in 1920 and three years later the club moved to the newly built Maine Road venue. Maine Road was a stadium located in Moss Side, Manchester, and was home to Man

City between 1923 and 2003. It was an all-seat venue by 2002-03, with a capacity of 35,150 for soccer, and had been renovated several times. Previously, the stadium could hold a maximum of 84,569.

5. The City of Manchester Stadium (Etihad Stadium) currently has a capacity of 55,017 for soccer. This makes it the sixth-largest venue in the Premier League and tenth largest in the UK. The stadium was originally constructed to host the 2002 Commonwealth Games. Man City agreed to lease the ground from the Manchester City Council in the summer of 2003 and then moved there from Maine Road. The ground was then demolished in 2004.

6. The record attendance for a Man City game at the Etihad Stadium game is 54,693 against Leicester City on Feb. 6, 2016. The record for a Man City contest at Maine Road match was 84,569 against Stoke City in the sixth round of the FA Cup on March 3, 1934.

7. A Wartime League was created during World War II, with Man City competing in the Northern Division. Since Manchester United's Old Trafford stadium was damaged during the war, Man United played numerous home games at Maine Road from 1945 to 1949 and again in 1956-57. Of course, Man City took over the home team dressing room when the two teams squared off against each other.

8. The club's home colors are sky blue and white while the away colors have typically been either maroon or red and

95

black stripes, similar to AC Milan. However, several other colors have been worn over the years. The club has also worn several different badges with the latest version being introduced in 2016.

9. Since 2003, Man City hasn't issued No. 23 to any of its players. The number was retired in memory of Marc-Vivien Foé, who was on loan from Lyon of France when he passed away during a game while playing for Cameroon in the 2003 FIFA Confederations Cup. The midfielder was just 28 years old when he collapsed on the pitch.

10. Manchester City Women's Football Club was formerly known as Manchester City Ladies FC The team currently competes in the FA Women's Super League and is affiliated with Manchester City FC The team's most common nicknames are the Citizens, the Blues, City, and Man City. It was founded in November 1988. Home games are played at the Academy Stadium in Manchester, which has a capacity of 7,000.

CHAPTER 10:

DOMESTIC COMPETITION

QUIZ TIME!

1. How many domestic trophies has Man City won as of 2020?

   a. 20

   b. 26

   c. 32

   d. 40

2. Man City has been runners-up for the FA Cup 8 times as of 2020.

   a. True

   b. False

3. The team defeated which side to win its first FA Cup?

   a. Bolton Wanderers

   b. Sheffield Wednesday FC

   c. Derby County FC

   d. Aston Villa

4. In which year did Man City win its first FA Charity/ Community Shield?

   a. 1972
   b. 1968
   c. 1937
   d. 1904

5. Which player scored the game-winning goal in the 2010-11 FA Cup final?

   a. Edin Džeko
   b. James Milner
   c. Carlos Tevez
   d. Yaya Touré

6. How many times has Man City won the First Division/ Premier League as of 2020?

   a. 3
   b. 5
   c. 7
   d. 10

7. In 2018-19, Man City became the first English men's team to win a domestic treble.

   a. True
   b. False

8. Man City beat which outfit in the 1969-70 League Cup final?

   a. West Bromwich Albion
   b. Birmingham City FC

c. Leicester City FC

d. Carlisle United

9. The club's highest home attendance of 84,569 was set in 1934 against which side?

    a. Peterborough United

    b. Stoke City

    c. Manchester United

    d. Barcelona

10. Man City faced which club in the 1985-86 Full Members' Cup final?

    a. Manchester United

    b. Tottenham Hotspur

    c. Liverpool FC

    d. Chelsea FC

11. When did Man City win its first League Cup?

    a. 1952-53

    b. 1963-64

    c. 1969-70

    d. 1975-76

12. Man City has won 7 second-tier titles as of 2020.

    a. True

    b. False

13. The club went head-to-head with which team in the 2015-16 League Cup final?

    a. Stoke City FC

    b. Everton FC

c. Manchester United

d. Liverpool FC

14. Who did Man City play in the 2014 FA Community Shield?

    a. Aston Villa

    b. Tottenham Hotspur

    c. Arsenal FC

    d. Chelsea FC

15. Which player was named Man of the Match in the 2015-16 League Cup final?

    a. Vincent Kompany

    b. Raheem Sterling

    c. Willy Caballero

    d. Fernandinho

16. Man City has won 8 League Cup trophies as of 2020.

    a. True

    b. False

17. Who scored the winning goal in the 2019-20 League Cup final?

    a. İlkay Gündoğan

    b. Rodri

    c. Sergio Agüero

    d. Raheem Sterling

18. How many times has Man City finished as FA Cup runner-up as of 2020?

a. 11

b. 8

c. 6

d. 4

19. Who was named Man of the Match in the 2019 FA Cup final?

   a. Ederson

   b. Gabriel Jesus

   c. Raheem Sterling

   d. Kevin De Bruyne

20. Man City won three consecutive League Cups between 2017 and 2019.

   a. True

   b. False

QUIZ ANSWERS

1. C – 32

2. B – False

3. A – Bolton Wanderers

4. C – 1937

5. D – Yaya Touré

6. C – 7

7. A – True

8. A – West Bromwich Albion

9. B – Stoke City

10. D – Chelsea FC

11. C – 1969-70

12. A – True

13. D – Liverpool FC

14. C – Arsenal FC

15. A – Vincent Kompany

16. B – False

17. B – Rodri

18. C – 6

19. D – Kevin De Bruyne

20. A – True

DID YOU KNOW?

1. Man City's biggest rivalry is with crosstown neighbors Manchester United. The games between the two teams are known as the Manchester Derby. The club also has less intense rivalries with Chelsea, Tottenham Hotspur, and Liverpool. The rivalry with Liverpool peaked in 2018-19 when Man City won the Premier League title over Liverpool by a single point. The team also has local rivalries with lower-tier teams Bolton Wanderers, Stockport County, and Oldham Athletic.

2. Man City is one of the most successful clubs in England, with 26 major domestic trophies to its name. The first major silverware won was the 1903-04 FA Cup but, before that, the side had captured three Manchester Cups. The first top-flight league won was the 1936-37 First Division and the first FA Community Shield came a few months later. The first League Cup was won in 1969-70 season and the squad also won the European Cup Winners' Cup. In 2018-19, City became the first side to win all four major English trophies, the Premier League, FA Cup, League Cup, and FA Community Shield.

3. The club has won the First Division of the Premier League six times as of 2020 while finishing as runners-up another six times. Their victories came in 1936-37, 1967-68, 2011-12, 2013-14, 2017-18, and 2018-19. They finished as

runners-up in 1903-04, 1920-21, 1976-77, 2012-13, 2014-15, and 2019-20.

4. Man City captured the FA Cup half a dozen times, in 1903-04, 1933-34, 1955-56, 1968-69, 2010-11, and 2018-19. They also lost five finals as they were runners-up in 1925-26, 1932-33, 1954-55, 1980-81, and 2012-13.

5. The side has celebrated seven League Cup titles, in 1969-70, 1975-76, 2013-14, 2015-16, 2017-18, 2018-19, and 2019-20. Man City has been quite successful when reaching the final of this competition, winning seven out of eight. The only defeat in a League Cup final came in 1973-74.

6. When it comes to the FA Community and Charity Shield, the team has won and lost it six times each. Their victories took place in 1937, 1968, 1972, 2012, 2018, and 2019, with the defeats coming in 1934, 1956, 1969, 1973, 2011, and 2014.

7. Man City shares the record for the most second-tier titles won with Leicester City at seven. The championships came in 1898-99, 1902-03, 1909-10, 1927-28, 1946-47, 1965-66, and 2001-02. They placed as runners-up in 1895-96, 1950-51, 1988-89, and 1999-2000. The team also earned promotion in 1984-85 when they finished in third place in the Second Division. In addition, they earned promotion in 1998-99 when they were the playoff winners of the third-tier Second Division and were runners-up in the division when it was the second tier 1895-96, 1950-51, and 1988-89.

8. The 1998-99 Second Division playoff final between Man City and Gillingham was one of the most dramatic ever played. The game took place at Wembley Stadium, with 76,935 fans in attendance. Gillingham took the lead in the 81st minute and then doubled it just five minutes later, causing many City fans to leave the ground. Kevin Horlock then scored for City in the 90th minute and Paul Dickov equalized after six minutes and nine seconds of injury time. The game was still 2-2 after 30 minutes of extra time. City won a penalty shootout 3-1 when goalkeeper Nicky Weaver saved two Gillingham penalties.

9. Between 1891-92 and 2019-20, Man City has been relegated 11 times, in the following seasons: 1901-02, 1908-09, 1925-26, 1937-38, 1949-50, 1962-63, 1983-83, 1986-87, 1995-96, 1997-98, and 2000-01. Nine of the relegations saw the club leave the top-tier level First Division or Premier League for the second-tier Second Division or First Division. In 1997-98, they were relegated from the second-tier First Division to the third-tier Second Division. The tiers were altered with the introduction of the Premier League in 1992-93.

10. The most points Man City has earned in a season in which three points are awarded for a win is 100, which they achieved in the 2017-18 Premier League. The most league goals scored in a campaign is 108, which they posted in 42 games in the Second Division in 1926-27. They equaled that mark in the First Division in 2001-02 in 46 games. The

most goals tallied in all competitions in a season was 169 in 2018-19. The team's record league victory and biggest margin of victory were 11-3 over Lincoln City in 1895 and 10-0 against Darwen in 1899. The biggest FA Cup win was 12-0 over Liverpool Stanley in 1890.

CHAPTER 11:

EUROPE AND BEYOND

QUIZ TIME!

1. How many trophies has Man City won in UEFA tournaments as of 2020?

   a. 0
   b. 1
   c. 5
   d. 8

2. The European Cup was the first international tournament Man City competed in.

   a. True
   b. False

3. Man City was eliminated by which club in the 1978-79 UEFA Europa League quarter-finals?

   a. Budapest Honvéd FC
   b. Arsenal FC
   c. Borussia Mönchengladbach
   d. Red Star Belgrade

4. Which club did Man City not face in the 1970-71 European Cup Winners' Cup?

    a. Górnik Zabrze
    b. Linfield FC
    c. Budapest Honvéd FC
    d. Real Madrid

5. How many times has the club won in the UEFA Champions League as of 2020?

    a. 0
    b. 1
    c. 3
    d. 4

6. Man City was eliminated by what team in the semifinals of the 1970-71 UEFA Cup Winners' Cup?

    a. Real Madrid
    b. Chelsea FC
    c. Budapest Honvéd FC
    d. FC Barcelona

7. Man City withdrew from the 1978 UEFA Europa Cup to focus on domestic competition.

    a. True
    b. False

8. Which player scored 2 goals in the second leg against Aalborg BK to send the team to the quarter-finals of the 2008-09 UEFA Europa League?

    a. Darius Vassell
    b. Felipe Caicedo

c. Craig Bellamy

d. Dietmar Hamann

9. What club did Man City beat in the 2015-16 UEFA Champions League quarter-final?

   a. Paris Saint-Germain

   b. Dynamo Kyiv

   c. Real Madrid

   d. Bayern Munich

10. Man City did not face this side in the 1975-76 Anglo-Scottish Cup.

    a. Sheffield United

    b. Blackpool FC

    c. Blackburn Rovers

    d. Oldham Athletic

11. Which squad did Man City beat in the 1969-70 European Cup Winners' Cup final?

    a. PSV Eindhoven

    b. FC Schalke 04

    c. AS Roma

    d. Górnik Zabrze

12. Man City faced Bologna FC in the 1969-1970 Anglo-Italian Cup final.

    a. True

    b. False

13. How many times has the club participated in the UEFA Europa League as of 2020?

a. 14

b. 10

c. 7

d. 5

14. Who scored the winning goal in the 1969-70 European Cup Winners' Cup final?

    a. Francis Lee

    b. Mike Doyle

    c. Alan Oakes

    d. Neil Young

15. In 2020, the club was originally banned from playing in European competitions for how many years?

    a. 1

    b. 2

    c. 4

    d. 5

16. Man City was banned from the Texaco Cup for five years after a betting scandal in 1972-73.

    a. True

    b. False

17. Which club defeated Man City in the 2019-20 UEFA Champions League quarter-final?

    a. Atalanta

    b. Olympique Lyon

    c. FC Porto

    d. Liverpool FC

18. Man City played which side in the 1971-72 Texaco Cup?

   a. Waterford FC

   b. Dundee United

   c. Shamrock Rovers

   d. Airdrieonians FC

19. Man City faced what team in its first European Cup match?

   a. Fenerbahçe SK

   b. Athletic Bilbao

   c. FC Twente

   d. Valencia CF

20. The fewest points Man City earned in a UEFA Champions League group stage as of 2020 was zero in 2012-13.

   a. True

   b. False

QUIZ ANSWERS

1. B – 1

2. A – True

3. C – Borussia Mönchengladbach

4. D – Real Madrid

5. A –0

6. B – Chelsea FC

7. B – False

8. C – Craig Bellamy

9. A – Paris Saint-Germain

10. D – Oldham Athletics

11. D – Górnik Zabrze

12. A – True

13. C – 7

14. A – Francis Lee

15. B – 2

16. B – False

17. B – Olympique Lyon

18. D – Airdrieonians FC

19. A – Fenerbahçe SK

20. b – False

DID YOU KNOW?

1. When it comes to European competition, Man City's lone triumph as of 2020 was capturing the 1969-70 European Cup Winners' Cup. The club also reached the semifinals of the European Champions League in 2015-16, where they were ousted 1-0 on aggregate by Real Madrid. They drew the first leg 0-0 at home and lost the second outing 1-0 away to the eventual champions.

2. The 1969-70 European Cup Winner's Cup final took place in Vienna, with Man City taking on Górnik Zabrze of Poland on April 19, 1970, with just 7,968 fans in the stands. City had beaten Athletic Bilbao (Spain), Lierse (Belgium), Académica (Portugal), and Schalke 04 (Germany) on the way to the final. Neil Young gave City a 12th-minute lead Francis Lee doubled that via a penalty kick two minutes before halftime. Górnik Zabrze made it 2-1 in the 68th minute but City hung on for the win.

3. Man City has represented England in the European Cup Champions League nine times while playing in the UEFA Cup/Europa League on seven occasions. The club also competed in the now-defunct European/UEFA Cup Winners' Cup twice. As of 2020, the side is one of 12 English clubs to win a European competition trophy.

4. The first time Man City competed on the continent was in 1968 when they entered the European Cup as the reward

for winning the 1967-68 First Division title. Things didn't go too well, though, as they lost to Fenerbahçe of Turkey in the first round. City drew the first leg 0-0 at home and was then edged 2-1 in Turkey to go down 2-1 on aggregate.

5. After winning the European Cup Winners' Cup, Man City reached the semifinal of the same competition the very next season but lost 2-0 on aggregate by fellow English side and eventual champions Chelsea. City dropped both the home and away legs 1-0. Until City qualified for Europe again in 2003, 24 years had passed since its last UEFA competition. However, in the 1970s, the team also competed in several non-UEFA-sanctioned tournaments in Europe, including the Texaco Cup and Anglo-Italian League Cup.

6. After winning the 1970 League Cup, Man City qualified for the Anglo-Italian League Cup against Bologna, which had won the previous season's Coppa Italia. City was beaten 1-0 in Bologna before drawing 2-2 at home to lose the competition 3-2 on aggregate.

7. When Man City failed to qualify for the 1971-72 UEFA Cup, the side was invited to compete in the Texaco Cup, which was a competition for English, Irish, and Scottish clubs. City fielded a weakened squad for the second leg of its first-round tie against Airdrieonians of Scotland after drawing the first leg 2-2 at home. The club was punished after losing the match 2-0 and its £1,000 participation

money was withheld. City was then banned from the competition for the next two years.

8. Man City entered the Texaco Cup event again in 1974-75 but was eliminated in the group stage after playing fellow English sides Blackpool, Sheffield United, and Oldham Athletic. They drew 1-1 at Blackpool, lost 4-2 at Sheffield, and won 2-1 at home over Oldham. When the Irish teams withdrew from the competition, it was renamed the Anglo-Scottish Cup in 1975-76. City played in the event that season but failed to progress from the group stage after losing 1-0 away to Blackpool and Blackburn Rovers and downing Sheffield United 3-1 at home.

9. As of January 2021, Man City's overall record in the European Cup Champions League stood at 45 wins, 17 draws, and 25 losses, with a plus-65 goal differential and a 51.72 winning percentage. The club's mark in the UEFA Cup/Europa League was 28 wins, 13 draws, and 11 losses with a plus-33 goal differential for a 53.85 winning percentage. its record in the European/UEFA Cup Winners' Cup was 11 wins, 2 draws, and 5 losses with a plus-19 goal differential for a 61.11 winning percentage. The total stood at 84 wins, 32 draws, and 41 losses with a plus 117 goal differential and a 53.50 winning percentage.

10. In July 2020, Man City's two-year suspension from European competition was overturned by the Court of Arbitration for Sport. The team was banned for allegedly breaching UEFA's Financial Fair Play by disguising equity

funding as sponsorship. In addition, the club's fine for failing to cooperate with UEFA was lowered from €30 million to € 10 million. The side had been banned five months earlier.

CHAPTER 12:

TOP SCORERS

QUIZ TIME!

1. Which player led the team with 10 goals in the Alliance League?

    a. David Weir

    b. Hugh Morris

    c. Jack Angus

    d. Bob Milarvie

2. Denis Law scored 6 goals against Luton Town, setting the current record for most goals scored in one game in any competition.

    a. True

    b. False

3. How many goals did Tommy Johnson score in 5 games with England?

    a. 0

    b. 4

    c. 5

    d. 8

4. Who was the first player to lead Man City in scoring in the Football League's Second Division?

    a. Billy Meredith
    b. Pat Finnerhan
    c. Billie Gillespie
    d. David Weir

5. Who is the club's all-time leading goal scorer in all competitions as of 2020?

    a. Tommy Johnson
    b. Colin Bell
    c. Sergio Agüero
    d. Eric Brook

6. How many goals did David White score to lead the squad in its inaugural Premier League season?

    a. 10
    b. 14
    c. 16
    d. 20

7. Frank Roberts was the first player to win a Golden Boot with Man City when he scored 31 times in the league in 1924-25.

    a. True
    b. False

8. This player led Man City to the 1936-37 First Division trophy with 30 goals.

    a. Fred Tilson
    b. Eric Brook

c. Alec Herd

d. Peter Doherty

9. How many goals did Colin Bell score in all competitions with the club?

   a. 162

   b. 153

   c. 147

   d. 139

10. Which player led the side with 20 goals in the 2019-20 domestic league?

   a. Raheem Sterling

   b. Gabriel Jesus

   c. Sergio Agüero

   d. Riyad Mahrez

11. How many goals did Uwe Rösler score in the 1993-94 Premier League?

   a. 22

   b. 15

   c. 13

   d. 9

12. The current club record for most goals scored in a season in all competitions is held by Fred Tilson with 38 in 1928-29.

   a. True

   b. False

13. How many goals did Billy Meredith score in his two stints with the club?

    a. 130
    b. 142
    c. 152
    d. 160

14. Who won the Golden Boot with 20 goals in 2010-11?

    a. Mario Balotelli
    b. Adam Johnson
    c. Carlos Tevez
    d. Yaya Touré

15. Which player led Man City with 14 goals in the 2012-13 Premier League?

    a. Sergio Agüero
    b. James Milner
    c. Carlos Tevez
    d. Edin Džeko

16. As of 2020, Sergio Agüero has scored over 250 goals in all competitions with Man City.

    a. True
    b. False

17. How many hat tricks had Sergio Agüero scored in domestic league matches as of January 2020?

    a. 14
    b. 11
    c. 16
    d. 12

18. Which player won a 1971-72 Golden Boot with 33 goals?

    a. Francis Lee

    b. Colin Bell

    c. Rodney Marsh

    d. Dennis Tueart

19. How many goals did Eric Brook score in all competitions?

    a. 177

    b. 164

    c. 150

    d. 146

20. Tommy Browell once scored 4 goals in a game and 5 goals in a game.

    a. True

    b. False

QUIZ ANSWERS

1. B – Hugh Morris

2. A – True

3. c – 5

4. D – David Weir

5. C – Sergio Agüero

6. C – 16

7. A – True

8. D – Peter Doherty

9. B – 153

10. A – Raheem Sterling

11. B – 15

12. B – False

13. C – 152

14. C – Carlos Tevez

15. D – Edin Džeko

16. A – True

17. D – 12

18. A – Francis Lee

19. A – 177

20. A – True

DID YOU KNOW?

1. Billy Gillespie enjoyed eight years with Man City and helped the side win a pair of Second Division titles and the FA Cup. The forward formed a fine partnership with Billy Meredith, who provided endless crosses for Gillespie to convert. And convert he did, scoring 132 goals in his 231 appearances. He arrived at the club in 1897 from Lincoln City and contributed 30 goals in 33 contests in 1902-03, including a streak of 27 goals in games. He notched another 21 markers in 30 outings the following campaign and then hung up his boots in 1905 and headed to South Africa.

2. Another player to tally 132 goals was center-forward Fred Tilson. He played with Man City from 1928 to 1938 and appeared in 273 contests. He missed numerous games due to injury but still managed a goal approximately every two outings on average. Tilson formed a superb partnership with Eric Brook at Barnsley and Man City was smart enough to buy both players for £6,000. It proved to be a brilliant move, as they combined for over 300 goals during the next decade and played close to 800 games combined. Tilson helped the side win the FA Cup and the First Division title before leaving for Northampton Town. He was inducted into the Man City Hall of Fame.

3. Tommy Browell was a 5-foot-8-inch center-forward who joined the team in 1913 from Everton end remained until leaving for Blackpool in 1926. He scored 139 times in 247 matches with Man City to justify his £1,780 transfer fee. Browell netted 13 goals in 27 starts in 1913-14 but World War I meant a four-year break after his second season with the club. Returning to action in 1919-20, Browell posted 22 goals and 31 the next campaign as the team finished runners-up in the First Division. He notched eight hat tricks for the squad, including 4 goals in one game and 5 in another.

4. English international forward Francis Lee signed in 1967 from Bolton Wanderers for £60,000. He was a lethal scorer and expert penalty-taker, with 15 goals coming from the spot one season to set an English League record and earn him the nickname "Lee One Pen." He netted 148 goals in 330 games and led the side in scoring for five straight seasons before being sold to Derby County in 1974. Lee won a First Division crown, FA Cup, League Cup, and European Cup Winners' Cup with Man City. He was inducted into the English Football Hall of Fame and later became a major shareholder and chairman of Man City for four years. He also trained racehorses.

5. Welsh international winger Billy Meredith had two stints with Man City, and he played with Manchester United in between. He racked up 152 goals in 394 games with City but moved to United with several of his teammates due to an illegal payment and bribe scandal. His first stint lasted

from 1894 to 1906 and he returned to the club from 1921 to 1924 before retiring. He's the oldest player to appear for the team at 49 years and 245 days of age. Meredith captained the side to its first FA Cup win in 1904 and helped it win the Second Division in 1898-99. He was later inducted into the English Football Hall of Fame and helped organize the player's union.

6. Forward Joe Hayes kicked off his pro career with Man City from 1953 to 1965 before joining Barnsley. He played 364 matches and tallied 152 goals, but a serious knee injury caused him to leave. He was an excellent poacher who helped the team win the 1955-1956 FA Cup. Hayes pocketed four goals during his trial game at Maine Road and made his first-team debut just two months later when he was 17 years old. Hayes suffered his injury in 1963 and appeared in only two more matches over the following 18 months before leaving.

7. Between 1966 and 1979, English international midfielder Colin Bell appeared in 501 games with Man City and produced 153 goals. He joined from Bury for £45,000 and helped the side win the Second Division in 1965-66. Bell went on to win seven other trophies. The club's Player of the Year for 1968, he was named to the PFA Football League Division 1 Team of the Year for 1974–75. He's also in the English Football Hall of Fame. Nicknamed "Nijinsky," Bell left in 1979 to play briefly in America and later became a reserve and youth coach team with Man City. Bell passed away in January 2021.

8. With five goals in five games for England, Tommy Johnson was a natural goal scorer, as he also showed at Man City between 1919 and 1930 with 166 goals in 354 outings. He holds the club's record for league goals in a season with 38 in 1928-29. The forward scored on his debut but didn't become a regular starter for another three years when he formed a fine partnership with Horace Barnes. Johnson helped the side win the Second Division in 1926-27 but moved to Everton for £6,000 in 1930 and helped them beat Man City in the 1933 FA Cup final.

9. In 1940, Eric Brook became Man City's all-time leading scorer with 177 goals to his name in 494 games after joining in 1928 from Barnsley. The durable English international forward stood just 5-feet, 6-inches tall but possessed a thunderous shot and was an expert penalty-taker. Brook was a consistent scorer who reached double figures in goals for 11 straight seasons but retired in 1940 after an auto accident. He helped his team win the FA Cup in 1933-34, the First Division title in 1936-37, and the 1937 FA Community Shield. Brook is also a member of the Manchester City Hall of Fame.

10. Surpassing Eric Brook as the club's all-time leading scorer in 2017 was Argentine international striker Sergio Agüero. After tallying 100 goals for Atlético Madrid from 2006 to 2011, the 23-year-old was bought by Man City for what was then a club-record fee of a reported £35 million. Agüero became a legend in his first campaign by scoring against Queens Park Rangers in the season finale to win

the 2011-12 Premier League title. He's helped the club win 13 trophies and has won numerous individual awards, including the 2014-15 Golden Boot. Although he's been somewhat injury prone, Agüero was still with City in 2020-21 and had 256 goals in 379 games.

CONCLUSION

You've just read through 14 decades' worth of fascinating Manchester City history from 1880 right up to 2021. We've delivered it in a fun fashion, and we hope you've also found the information and facts to be educational as well.

We've included the cup triumphs and disappointments, along with the relegations, league championships, record transfers, and numerous other facts and team records.

With such a long and storied history, it's impossible to include each and every member of the club and we hope we haven't left out your favorites.

Equipped with 12 unique chapters that are filled with quiz questions and a multitude of "Did You Know" facts and anecdotes, you should now be well prepared to challenge fellow Man City fans and others to an array of different quiz contests to see who knows the most about this remarkable sports organization.

We also hope you'll be inclined to share this trivia and fact book with others to help spread the word about the club's long history to those who may not be aware of it.

There's still a long way to go when it comes to the Man City story and it appears the club is on the verge of setting new soccer milestones and records in the next leg of its journey.

Thank you kindly for proving to be a true Man City fan by reading this trivia book and reliving the club's history every step of the way.

Printed in Great Britain
by Amazon

23810741R00076